Learning Swimming

Barth/Dietze

Sport Science Consultant:
Dr. Berndt Barth

Meyer & Meyer Sport

Original Title: Ich lerne Schwimmen
Aachen: Meyer & Meyer 2002
Translated by Susanne Evens, Petra Haynes
AAA Translation, St. Louis, Missouri, USA
www.AAATranslation.com

British Library Cataloguing in Publication Data
A catalogue record for this book is available from the British Library

Learning Swimming
Katrin Barth / Jürgen Dietze
Oxford: Meyer & Meyer Sport (UK) Ltd., 2004
ISBN 1-84126-144-0

© 2004 by Meyer & Meyer Sport (UK) Ltd.
Aachen, Adelaide, Auckland, Budapest, Graz, Johannesburg,
Miami, Olten (CH), Oxford, Singapore, Toronto
Member of the World
Sports Publishers' Association (WSPA)
www.w-s-p-a.org
Printed and bound by: FINIDR, s. r. o., Český Těšín
ISBN 1-84126-144-0
E-Mail: verlag@m-m-sports.com
www.m-m-sports.com

......................TABLE OF CONTENTS

The exercises and practical suggestions in this book have been carefully chosen and reviewed by the authors. However, the authors are not liable for accidents or damage of any kind incurred in connection with this book.

You will frequently see pictures of Dolly in this book

This means Dolly has a tip or an important suggestion to help you do even better.

Here are exercises you can do in the pool or at the lake with Mom, Dad, Grandmother, Grandfather, or your siblings.

Here Dolly is shown in a house, which means she is at home. Next to this picture will be exercises you can do without a large swimming pool.

Sometimes Dolly has an exercise or a puzzle for you to do. You will find these next to the question mark. The answers are in the back of the book.

If you see Dolly with a pencil it means there is something to color in or to write down. If you like you can color in all the drawings in the book.

Some of the exercises aren't all that easy to do and you have to have some courage. Congratulations and bravo if you try something and succeed! As a reward you get to color Dolly's flower.

MY LITTLE SWIMMING JOURNAL

I received this book on: _____

The first time I went to

- *an indoor swimming pool:* _____
- *an outdoor swimming pool:* _____
- *the beach:* _____

My favorite person to go swimming with is: _____

The first time I jumped into shallow water: date: _____

The first time I jumped into deep water: date: _____

The first time I dove into the water: date: _____

I am learning to swim at: _____

The name of my swimming instructor is: _____

My first swimming lesson was on: _____

The first time I swam alone was on: _____

How I like swimming: ☺   🙂   ☹

....................................1 LET'S TALK

Dear beginning Swimmer,

Some kids are tall and some are short, some are big, some are thin, or loud, or quiet. Some kids like to draw, do puzzles, or crafts. Some like to go wild on the playground, climb trees, or get into a tussle. The skilled ball player will soon join a soccer team, the good singer will join a choir, and the clown will join a children's theater group. Every child has different talents. That means that every child is really good at something and has fun doing it.

What do you like to do most?

_____

Have you already joined a children's group or a team?

_____

In the beginning swimming is not a recreational activity like riding a bike, playing soccer, dancing, singing, or playing tennis. Everyone needs to know how to swim!

Every baby learns to walk during the first year of life because it can't ride around in a stroller forever. Toddlers want to learn how to talk so they can finally say what it is they want. Later on at school all children learn to read, write, and do math.

But why do we have to learn to swim?

So you don't go under while you are bathing or playing in the water. Swimming can save your life. Every year children and grown-ups drown because they can't swim or can't swim very well. By learning to swim and knowing how to behave in the water you can protect yourself.

What else is swimming good for?

Spending time in cool water toughens your body, which will protect you from getting colds. Moving in the water and breathing strengthens your heart and lungs. You improve your endurance, don't get tired as quickly, and strengthen your muscles. The body is lighter in water than on land. That's good for the spine, bones, and joints.

When you go swimming at the pool you meet other children. You'll have lots of fun swimming, playing ball, jumping, diving, and sliding, and you'll make new friends.

Once you have learned to swim and you enjoy it you can keep practicing. Maybe there is a swim team that meets regularly in your area. Successful swimmers who compete at big swimming competitions and win medals started out that way, too.

We have listed quite a few good and important reasons for learning to swim. Now it's time to get started!
The best time to start learning to swim is the year before you start school.

This book should accompany you as you learn to swim. We have included interesting facts about water, tips and tricks, as well as exercises. We'll also explain why some preliminary exercises in the water are so important, and what you need to be able to do.

If you are not reading yet, look at the pictures and have someone read to you. But this book isn't just for reading and looking at. You get to help design it. Record your dates, color in the illustrations, add photos, and do the puzzles and exercises. Just enjoy the book and hurry up and learn to swim.

We hope you have lots of fun!

The authors ...

...and Dolly!

13

"Do you like dolphins, too?" You can use this page to draw dolphins or to paste down some beautiful photos of dolphins!"

"Finish drawing me!"

..................2 ABOUT THE HISTORY OF SWIMMING

Humans have always enjoyed bathing and swimming. Playing around in the water is fun, refreshing on hot days, and strengthens the body.

People liked to build their huts and houses near rivers, lakes, or the ocean. This provided a good view, fresh fish to eat, and with boats one could get comfortably from place to place. Before there were washing machines people did their laundry in clean rivers, and as you can imagine they washed their little children right along with it.

One night recently Dolly was already lying in bed, but she couldn't go to sleep. She still had to ask her mother an important question.

"Mom, who taught you how to swim?"
   "Your grandparents, Dolly."
"And who taught my grandparents how to swim?"
   "Your great-grandparents did."
"And who taught my great-grandparents how to swim?"
   "Your great-great-grandparents."
"And who taught my great-great-grandparents how to swim?"
   "Your great-great-great-grandparents."
"And who taught my great-great-great-grandparents how to swim?"
   "Your great-great-great-great-grandparents."
"And who taught ..."

You'll find out on the next page how the story ends.

Oops! Dolly has gone to sleep!

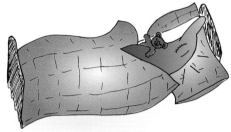

Romping in the water, splashing and squirting is particularly fun for children. But the water can also be dangerous. That is why parents everywhere have always made sure their little ones learn to swim as early as possible. Most of the time children learned to swim from other family members. Later there were actual swim instructors.

Different types of swim sports

As a swimmer you can swim at a leisurely pace. It's also really fun to have races with other swimmers. But being able to swim well is also important for a number of other sports.

Racing

There are different types of competitions where the swimming stroke and the racing distance have been predetermined. Who is the fastest swimmer?

Diving

The athletes jump off a high dive or a spring board at different heights. They do flips, twists, or other beautiful figures.

Synchronized swimming

It looks like the athletes are dancing to music in the water. Alone, in pairs, or as a group they do beautiful figures. They move through the water like ballet dancers.

Water polo

The pool is divided into a playing field with two goals. The players of both teams move around the field by swimming and try to score by throwing the ball in the opposing goal.

Surfing, sailing, rowing, and paddling

These athletes are on a surfboard or in a boat. But one awkward move and they can go overboard. All water athletes should be good swimmers!

Whenever non-swimmers get into a boat they must wear a swim-vest!

Swim lessons in the past and today

Anyone competing against other athletes in competitions wants to be good. That's why there have always been swimming instructors and trainers who work hard with the athletes.

More than a hundred years ago eager swimming instructors thought that the best method for learning to swim was to start with land exercises.

Before the beginning swimmers were allowed in the water they had to practice all of the arm- and leg movements on land, and master them perfectly. Many exercises were performed on a trestle or a high stool.

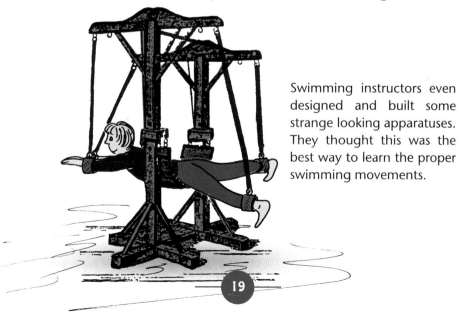

Swimming instructors even designed and built some strange looking apparatuses. They thought this was the best way to learn the proper swimming movements.

Nowadays these so called *dry exercises* are rarely done anymore. Sometimes the swimming instructor demonstrates how to do the arm- or leg movements from the edge of the pool, and then asks the children to repeat them. But the practicing is done in the water. Only there do we have the right conditions for swimming.

Swimming can only be learned by swimming!

.......3 HI THERE, NADINE!

Hey, wait a minute!
I'm Dolly, and I want to help children learn to swim!

Hi, Dolly! I'm Nadine and you don't need to help me.

I saw that. Can I ask you a few questions as an interview for my book about swimming?

Yeah, ok! Other kids would probably like to learn how to swim and maybe take swimming lessons.

You can already swim really fast, you fearlessly jump into deep water, and you can even dive under water. And you don't even go to school yet.

I learned all that in my swimming class along with my friends. Now I am allowed to get in the big pool with Mom.

It sounds so easy. Wasn't it difficult for you?

Yes, a little bit. Sometimes I was afraid I might get water in my eyes, or that I might go under.

And how did you become such a brave swimmer?

Our swimming instructors showed me how the water can bear a person's weight, how the body glides in the water, and how to breathe so I don't swallow water. Then I had to practice lots.

Did you always have fun?

Most of the time, but not always. The first time I jumped into deep water my swimming instructor had to be very patient with me. I got so much water in my mouth and up my nose that I just kept on coughing. I cried and wanted to quit that stupid swimming right then.

Did you?

No, my mom kept saying "You can do it!" The swimming instructor comforted me and Mom was there when I took the final test. I even practiced breathing with her at home in the bathtub.

What will you do next?

I am planning to keep practicing so I'll get more confident. Then I can show my brother Patrick that I'm a better swimmer than he is. In my next swimming class I will learn the backstroke. I think that'll be lots of fun.

Well, Nadine, you have big plans. I hope you'll continue to have lots of fun. See you soon, and thanks for the interview.

........................4 FIT AND HEALTHY

Most people doing sports want to have fun and be successful. One important goal in sports is to keep your body healthy and fit.

Eating right must be learned

When you do sports you use up more energy than a couch potato does. That's why food tastes best after swimming – because you are hungry!

Almost all kids like to eat chocolate, chips, fries, and pizza. That's not exactly a meal for athletes, especially if you eat these things often and in large quantities. These types of food contain too much fat.

Swimming lesson was great, but now I'm hungry!

A better meal to eat after swimming lessons would be whole grain bread, cheese, fruit, and yogurt. There are many foods that are healthy and taste good, too. Try to eat a variety of foods in moderate quantities.

If you sweat a lot you must drink regularly

Believe it or not, but even swimmers sweat. While you swim your body loses a lot of fluids which must be replenished by drinking sufficiently. The best thirst quenchers are water, fruit juice mixes (a mix of juice and water), or tea (you can sweeten it with honey).

Pure juice or sodas are not suitable as fluid replacements. They contain too much sugar. When you are thirsty and drink something, be careful not to drink too hastily. It is better to take small sips more frequently.

Make sure you don't fill up your stomach so much that you will barely be able to move. If you drink too much before a swimming lesson you'll float like a sack of sand.

 *Do not bring glass bottles to the pool! They break easily. Other people using the pool are walking around barefoot and might cut their feet on the glass.*

Alive and kicking

Children should get plenty of fresh air. They should run, climb, and play. It keeps them healthy and fit. That includes visits to the pool. But if you aren't quite as healthy, ask your doctor. Your pediatrician will explain to you and your parents, what you need to pay attention to when you visit the pool.

A successful day begins with a good start in the morning!

Some tips from Dolly!

- Go to bed on time and get plenty of sleep!

- Look forward to a new day.

- Stretch a little when you get up. How about some morning exercises?

- Finishing your shower with cold water is great. It's refreshing and makes you tough.

- Whole grain bread, cereal, milk, yogurt, and fruit are all part of a good and healthy breakfast.

- Don't forget to brush your teeth after you eat!

Speedster and Dolly are going fishing

..............................5 WHAT I NEED TO BRING TO THE POOL

You don't need much for swimming, and you probably won't even have to buy the most important things. A swimming suit, flip flops, a towel, and shampoo, – and you're ready to go!

> Hey, Dolly! Wake up! I need to pack my swim bag.

Swimming attire

Every visitor to the pool wears a swimming suit or a pair of swimming trunks. This clothing should fit well and not be bothersome when you are swimming. Swimming attire is often made from a special fabric that doesn't absorb too much water. Wet baggy clothing is too heavy and interferes with your ability to move.

Many years ago fashionable swim wear was quite different. Can you imagine getting in the water dressed like these two children?

Swimming cap

At some pools you have to wear a swimming cap. This is to prevent loose hair getting in the water and clogging up the drain. Also, some swim instructors have the children in their lesson groups wear identically colored swimming caps, so the children will know exactly where they belong. To make it even easier they sometimes put their names on them.

Foot wear

Visitors to the pool take off their street shoes in the changing room so they don't carry any dirt into the pool area. If you bring a pair of water shoes or flip flops you won't slip as easily on the wet floor. They also protect your feet from infectious diseases such as fungal infections.

Goggles

Some swimmers wear goggles to protect their eyes from the chlorinated pool water.

What else you need

Of course, you have to shower before and after swimming. Just imagine some dirty person getting in the pool with you. Yuk!

After swimming you need to rinse off the chlorinated water really well. In the pool the chlorine protects you from diseases, but afterwards it could be harmful to your skin.

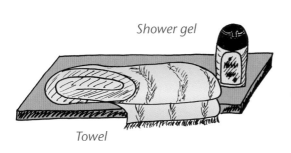

Shower gel

Towel

On cold days bring a hat so you don't catch a cold on the way home. Also, pack a snack because you'll be hungry after swimming.

Here is something for you to color.

............................6 THE WATER

*What do you think of
when you hear the word* water?

*Make a drawing, write it down, or
ask someone to write it down for you.*

You will find out what water made us think of on the solutions-and-answers page (see p. 115). Did you have the same ideas? Did we forget something important?

Which compound words begin with water? The drawings will help you.
If you can think of more write them down, or make a drawing.

32

What water can be like

Water can be soft and pleasant.

It is wet and sometimes rather cold.

Water is powerful, and it can be hard and dangerous.

Sea water is salty. Storms can create waves and currents which swimmers need to pay attention to.

If you want to learn to swim you need to know about water

You can do some experiments with water at home.

In the bathtub

You are lying in the bathtub, gently rocking side to side. Soon the water starts to move with you, and your body is rocking without your help. Be careful not to splash over the edge!

In the sink

Fill a sink with water and put a small ball in it. Open the drain. What do you see?

Water will bear your weight

This is great! I think I'll take a nap.

Of course it's not quite as easy as Dolly thinks. But have you noticed that all your movements are different in the water than on land?

Let yourself fall backwards in the pool and feel how the water catches you. In your living room you would hit the floor hard.

Try to run in the water and you will feel how the water slows down your movements.

Your mom has probably complained that you have gotten really heavy, and she can hardly carry you anymore. In the water you are light as a feather and mom can hold you with one hand.

An object must have certain properties to be able to float on water. Very light objects like a water noodle, a kick board, or a cork stay on the surface.

A ball filled with air, or an empty plastic bottle will also float.

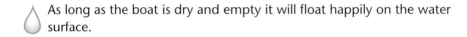

Here is an experiment with a paper boat. Try it!

💧 As long as the boat is dry and empty it will float happily on the water surface.

💧 If the little boat gets splashed, or the paper absorbs the water, it sinks lower and lower and threatens to go down.

💧 A soaking wet paper boat full of water is too heavy to float and sinks to the bottom.

Imagine yourself acting like a slightly wet paper boat. You don't go all the way under, but you also don't float on the surface. To stay on top you need to move a little, and the water will help you.

You can do this exercise in the pool. Do you notice how light your body is in the water? If you inhale your chest fills with air and it's even easier.

Sit down on the pool steps. Your body is under water up to your chin. Now try to straighten out by moving just a little.

In this drawing you can see the crouch float. This exercise is pretty difficult and requires some courage. Would you like to try it? Take a deep breath and let yourself drift like package.

Playing in the water

To enjoy swimming you have to feel comfortable in the water. Just like Dolly, who likes to splash in the water all day long. Here you will find some water games for shallow water.

- Play catch.
- If you have a ball, throw it to each other.
- It's also fun to splash each other. Whoever gives up first loses.

*Pretend you're a **crocodile**. In shallow water support yourself only with your hands and let your legs float. Now walk on your hands and try to catch the others.*

I'm the crocodile and I'm going to catch all the water snails.

Try all the different things you can do with a water noodle. The boy in the picture is trying to ride it.

Swimming aids

There are many swimming aids you can buy for playing in the water and learning to swim. You've probably already got one or the other as a gift. They help you stay above the water while you are learning to swim.

We drew some of the devices you can use for playing in the water, for getting used to the water, and while learning to swim. But in the end you have to be able to swim without aid.
So keep trying it to see how it feels.

*Color in the items
you already know!*

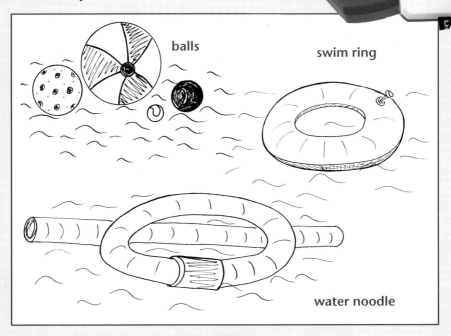

balls

swim ring

water noodle

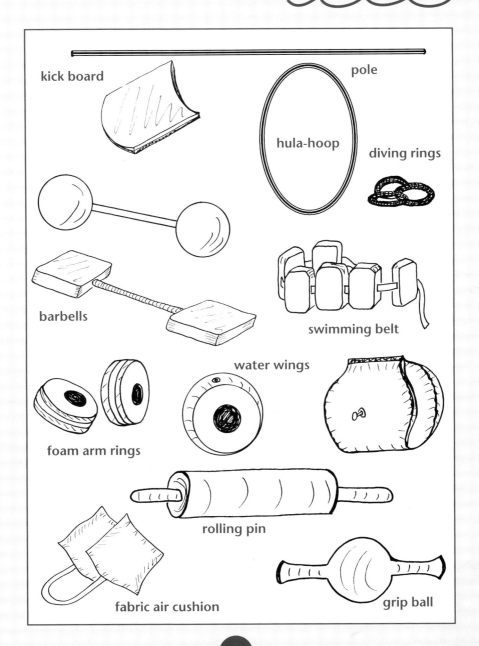

kick board

pole

hula-hoop

diving rings

barbells

swimming belt

foam arm rings

water wings

rolling pin

fabric air cushion

grip ball

41

LEARNING SWIMMING

What did we forget? Add your own drawing. Which swimming aid do you like to use in the water?

Swimming aids do not protect you from drowning. You should never get in deep water with a swimming aid if you don't know how to swim!

···········7 When do we learn to swim

In these drawings you can see what Dolly likes to do in and around the water.

Swimming and playing ball

Jumping and diving

Boating

Fishing

Ice skating on the frozen lake in winter

Do you enjoy doing these things, too? What do you like to do in and around the water?

Which animals are at the pond? Where's Dolly?
Which other animals live in or near the water?

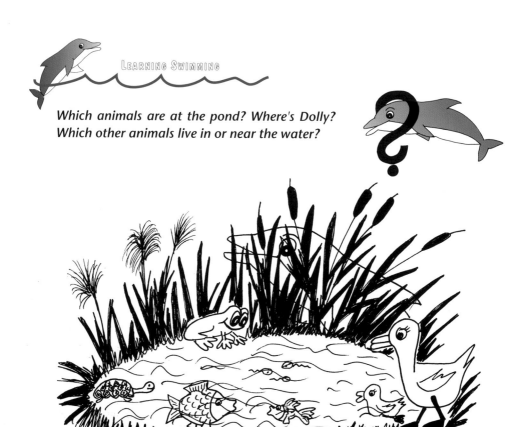

Fish, frogs, ducks, and many other animals live in or near the water. Of course so does Dolly. That's where they find their food and lay their eggs. The water is their home. That's the reason they are such good swimmers and divers, and some of them can even breathe under water. Living on land without water would make them very unhappy. The little fish, ducklings, and frogs swim right from the start. They are born in or near the water and can swim immediately.

Just like you, most people love the water. Many families spend their vacations at a lake or at the seaside. But humans really belong on dry land. Most babies like the water, but they don't know how to swim. Children learn to swim later.

Baby swimming and getting used to the water

Are you a super bathtub splasher, too? Does your mom have trouble getting you out of the tub? Many children like splashing, playing, diving, and blowing bubbles in warm water.

When moms, dads, or grandparents have time they like to take their babies or toddlers to the pool for baby swimming. Of course it's not really swimming, but they have lots of fun in the water. In the beginning the little ones find the big pool a little eerie, but they soon start enjoying all the exercises.

It is important to get used to being in the water before actually learning to swim. Some places don't have a nice pool for children, or their parents have to go to work and don't have the time. But some things you can try in the bathtub. You also don't need to be a baby to do the exercises on the following pages. You can do these exercises later at the pool or when you're on vacation.

Sailing, sailing, ...!

Even if children don't know how to swim, they still enjoy playing in the water.

Do you recognize these toys? Add drawings of your favorite toys.

First encounters with the "big water"

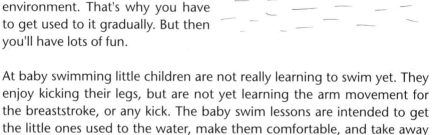

Do you remember your first time at the pool, the lake, or even the ocean? So much water! It's wet, splashy, and makes waves. Were you afraid of the water or did you jump right in? As you already know water is not a human's environment. That's why you have to get used to it gradually. But then you'll have lots of fun.

At baby swimming little children are not really learning to swim yet. They enjoy kicking their legs, but are not yet learning the arm movement for the breaststroke, or any kick. The baby swim lessons are intended to get the little ones used to the water, make them comfortable, and take away their fear.

When was the first time you were in "big water"?
Do you have a photo?
You can paste it here.

Big people help

There are many ways to hold someone. When a big person holds you in the water you should feel secure and not be afraid. Do what you enjoy and what makes you feel safe. If you don't cling to your mom like a little monkey you can even move your arms and legs. That's fun!

Snuggling in the water and being carried is the best.

The big person has his hand under the child's tummy and holds him securely. It's nice to be able to splash with your arms and legs this way.

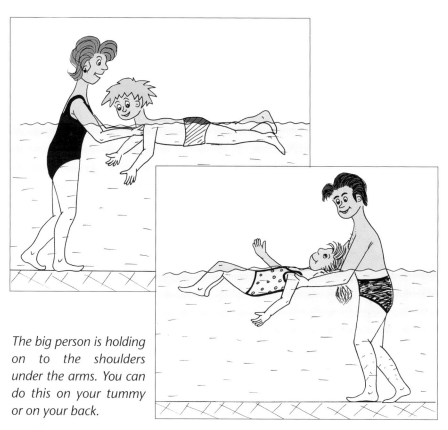

The big person is holding on to the shoulders under the arms. You can do this on your tummy or on your back.

That's fun!

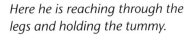

Here he is reaching through the legs and holding the tummy.

This child is only being held at the hips.

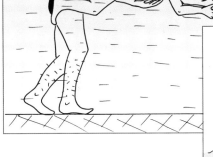

Now you can jump, swing, and twirl together in the water. Sing songs and slap the water with your hands. Are you afraid of getting splashed? How about emptying a cup of water on your head?

In addition to those swimming aids we've already talked about you can bring all kinds of other toys in the bathtub or the pool. They should be made of plastic or rubber. Your parents will know what is suitable, and what should not get wet.

Carefully look at this picture.
Which toys should you not take in the water?

Some tips from Dolly:

If your mom isn't sure if playing in the water is good for you she can ask the pediatrician.

Water is lots of fun for healthy children. Moving in the water is healthy and makes you strong.

For small children the water needs to be warm because they get cold more easily than big people do.

Children who can't swim should never get in deep water alone. Be careful at the edge of the pool because it may be slippery and you could fall in.

Don't get too wild and try too many tricks at one time. You don't want to become afraid of the water.

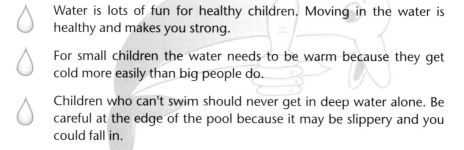

What is the right time for learning to swim?

All parents want their children to be able to swim at an early age. Then they don't have to worry as much when their children are near a pond, the pool, or the beach.

Babies can splash in the water and sometimes even put their heads under. But they can't swim yet. Their arms and legs are not strong enough, the coordinated movement is too difficult, and their heads are much too big and heavy.

We think the best time to learn to swim is right before school age, around the age of five. Of course some children start sooner. And there are children who learn to swim later. But it is never too late. Some grown-ups never had the time or opportunity as children It is great when they still learn it later! There are swimming instructors and classes for everyone.

The process is always the same:

○ *Getting used to the water by playing and having fun.*

○ *Learning the basic skills.*

○ *Learning technique.*

The first goal in learning to swim is to successfully complete a beginning course and receive a certificate of achievement. You will have to demonstrate that you can jump into deep water, that you can swim a certain distance, and that you can retrieve an object from the bottom of the pool in the shallow end. You also need to know the pool rules.

....................8 THE BASIC SKILLS

As a beginning swimmer there are some things you need to know before you start doing the actual swimming movements. The swimming instructor calls those *basic skills*. You need these basic skills to feel secure in the water and as preparation to the actual swimming movements.

What can you do already?
Mark it with an X.

☐ *Keeping your eyes open under water.*

☐ *Jumping into shallow water.*

☐ *Jumping into deep water.*

☐ *Surfacing by yourself.*

☐ *Putting your face in the water and blowing bubbles.*

☐ *Playing "dead man float".*

☐ *Being dragged through the water.*

☐ *Walking around in the water.*

☐ *Wearing water wings or a swim ring in deep water.*

Did you make a lot of checks? If not, it doesn't matter. You are just starting out. On the following page we'll explain about the basic skills, and how you can practice. *Have fun!*

Part of water safety is:

Swimming under water

Breathing

Jumping in

To swim you also need to be able to:

Glide

Move forward

Here we have illustrated and described a number of exercises for you. You can practice these alone, or with other children or grown-ups. If you have done a good job you can color in Dolly's flower.

Swimming under water

Why do you need to be able to swim under water?

When you swim in the ocean a big wave sometimes splashes you in the face. Or another child jumps on top of you in the pool. If you don't know how to swim under water you might be really startled and frightened. You'll cough and rub your eyes. If you have practiced swimming under water you'll know that getting a little water in your face isn't so bad. You'll also know that humans can stay under water for short periods of time and are even able to see.

No matter how you jump into the water, you'll always go under first due to your weight. So you go under water automatically. Some people feel really comfortable in the water. They can splash, jump, and dive all day. But some people find being splashed or even putting their head under water very unpleasant. How about you?

Regardless, if you are a little scared or a super bathtub diver, anyone who wants to be a good and safe swimmer can't be afraid to swim under water.

Part of swimming under water is fearlessly submerging and finding your way with your eyes open.

Here are a few under water exercises for shallow water

Keep your eyes open while you splash water in your face.

Ask someone to hold a hula-hoop under water. Now swim up to it and climb through it with your eyes open.

Put a water noodle, a kick board, or something similar on the water surface. Then swim under it with your eyes open.

Throw a diving ring, or another item that will sink into the water. Then pick it up. Keep your eyes open or you won't see anything!

Together with others you can play:

• Who gets the ring first?
• Who picks up the most rings?

Never push another person under water against his or her will!

And now a few exercises for deep water

Hold on to the edge of the pool, take a deep breath through the mouth, and then slowly go under water. When you exhale you can see the air bubbles. Now pull yourself back up.

If you're not ready to put your whole head under water try to do it a little bit at a time: first up to the mouth, then the nose, then the eyes, and then the entire head.

Who can do it the longest?

Let yourself sink straight to the bottom. When your feet touch the bottom, push off hard to get back to the surface.

Remember, – never practice alone in deep water!

Jumping in

Why do you have to be able to jump into the water?

When you jump into the water and then come back up you show that you are not afraid of the water. Then if you should ever fall into the water you won't get half as scared. You'll come back up and just laugh it off. Besides, at most swimming competitions jumping into the water marks the beginning of the race.

Jumping into the water means bravely jumping from an elevated point and safely surfacing.

Do these two exercises in shallow water where you can safely stand:

From the edge of the pool, jump into a hoop.

From the edge of the pool, jump over a small ball.

When you jump into deep water you'll first go under. That's obvious because you are heavy and have lots of momentum. But as you already know, the water helps you to surface. You move your arms and legs a little and you come back up. So, be brave! Besides, there is always someone with you who is watching and will pull you up if necessary.

These jumping exercises are for deep water

Take a big jump so you can reach the pole. You can hold on to it in the water. Be careful not to jump to the wall!

Bend your knees, reach back with your arms to get some momentum, and jump up and out. You can jump in with straight legs. If you want to get your friends wet, jump in with your legs drawn up. That will make a big splash.

If you're still a little scared the pole can be held in the water so you have something to hold onto as soon as you surface.

Diving in head first requires some courage

So try it from a sitting position first. Your hands point to the water and your head is between your arms. Place your feet on the spillway or against the pool wall. Now let yourself fall forward and push off with your feet.

Next try it on your knees.

Now you are ready to try the head first dive. That will become important as a starting dive.

Never jump into deep water if you don't know how to swim!

Breathing

Why do you have to breathe differently in the water?

That was probably one of the first things you discovered about being in the water. You swallowed water because you tried to inhale in the water.

Breathing without swallowing water really isn't that difficult. You just have to practice. Then it's almost automatic and you can pay more attention to your arms and legs.

What happens when you try to inhale under water? Right, – you swallow water. You have to practice breathing properly so that doesn't happen.

Part of breathing is:

Taking a deep breath through the mouth above water.

Deliberately exhaling through the mouth and nose in the water.

Regularly in- and exhaling while you are moving.

Here are a few exercises you can do in the water

Put a rubber duck in the water. By blowing against the duck try to propel it to the edge of the pool.

Take a deep breath and then exhale into the water. Watch the air bubbles rise. Try to blow for a really long time. How long can you do it?

These breathing exercises also work well in the bathtub.

Hold hands with someone else. Now take a deep breath, go under water, and exhale. Can you see the air bubbles rise to the surface?

Hold on to a kick board and kick your legs. Turn your head to the side to inhale, and exhale down into the water. How far can you go using this technique?

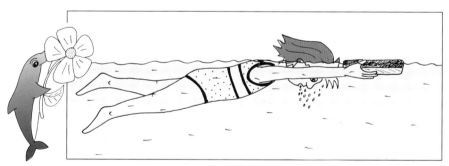

Now you can repeat all of the exercises for swimming under water with the correct breathing.

You can only inhale above water. You should exhale into the water.

67

Breathing in and out

Gliding

Why does a swimmer have to be able to glide?

Being able to do the swimming movements isn't enough. You need to be able to stay on the surface without going under. For that you need to know how to glide. If you stretch out very slowly on the water surface you can briefly lie on top of the water. It's as if it carries you.

You need to know this sensation before you can begin the actual swimming movements.

This includes being able to glide in the water for a distance on your stomach or your back, with arms and legs extended, after pushing off from the wall.

Some exercises

Playing "dead man float".

Take a deep breath and stretch out long on the water without moving. If you like you can start by holding on to something.

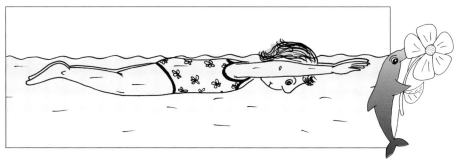

Now try it on your back.

Now try to flip from your stomach to your back, and back to your stomach while you are gliding.

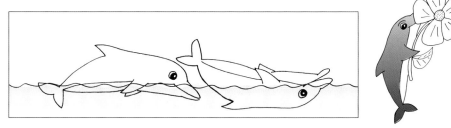

Have someone drag you through the water. Hold your face up, to the side, or in the water. Also try it on your back. How about going in a circle?

Try doing this exercise with other children. Be confident.

They won't let go of you!

Push off hard with your feet and glide as far as you can. You'll have to really stretch out. If you like use a kick board or barbells.

Try it on your stomach and on your back.
How far can you glide?

During the first exercise on your back hold your arms at your side.

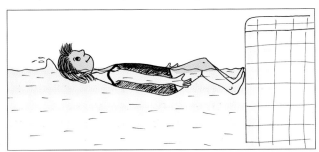

During the next exercise, reach back with your arms.

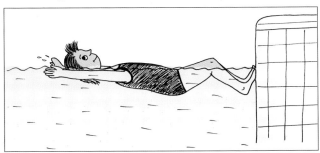

Moving forward

Why do you have to be able to keep moving in the water?

It is very important that you know all about water and are comfortable with it. Sometimes unexpected things can happen while you are swimming. Your hand starts to hurt and you can't move it any longer, you swallowed water, or some big waves are approaching. This can be frightening to children. That's when you need to remember other ways to keep moving. In shallow water you can walk or hold on to something and kick your legs.

Practice these forward movements if you have not yet learned a stroke.

Moving forward in the water means moving your arms and legs in such a way that you keep moving forward. Regular breathing is important here.

73

In **shallow water** you can walk. It takes a little more effort than walking down the street, but you will be able to move forward. If you use your hands to push the water back it's even easier.

Sit down at the edge of the pool and kick your legs really hard. Be careful not to fall in! Do you feel the water's resistance?

You know that you should never get in deep water alone. But if a swimmer is with you, try these exercises in **deep water**.

If you can hold on to the side of the pool move hand over hand along the edge of the pool. You can also do this to get from the deep end back to the shallow end of the pool, or to save yourself if you fall in.

With the swimming aids you can move around the pool quite independently. But remember, that's not really swimming! If you lose hold of the water noodle or the water wings deflate, you'll go under.

So, be careful and never get in deep water alone!

If you have a swimming aid like a swim ring, a kickboard, barbells, water wings, or a water noodle, you can paddle with your arms or legs. You'll be able to move forward like that.

You can get to the edge of the pool if you move your legs like you are walking.

Only two of the dolphins are identical!

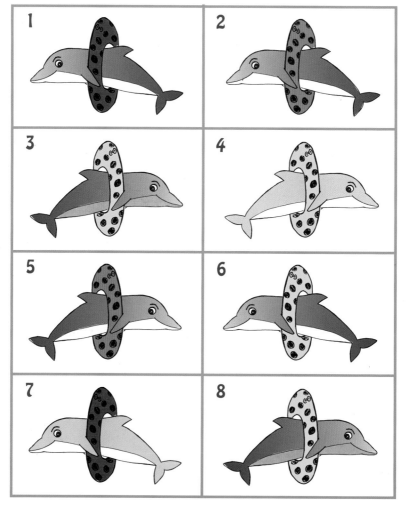

.......................9 THE BREASTSTROKE

You can actually pick any stroke for learning to swim. But most beginning swimmers choose to learn the breaststroke first. Did you? That's because most people prefer to swim in a face-down position. They are able to see their surroundings and are less afraid.

Your body floats well in a face-down position and that makes you feel more secure. Beginning swimmers using the breaststroke are able to swim longer and farther.

To swim without a hitch, it's true,
the flying boat position works for you!

The way Dolly's boat sits in the water is also the best position for a swimmer. Your body should be straight, a little higher in the front, a little lower in the back. It should be neither too shallow nor too vertical.

How to do the breaststroke – the technique

The breaststroke is a parallel stroke. Both arms and legs move evenly. The body lies in the water at an angle, just like a flying boat. The rear is a little lower than the shoulders.

For each arm movement there is a leg movement. When the hands and underarms are brought to the inside the tucking in of the legs begins. As the arms are extended the lower leg kick takes place.

The legs

The legs move simultaneously. The lower legs and feet do a kicking motion. This creates a strong push forward. For this the knees are held close together and the feet are pulled in to the rear. When the lower legs are in the straddle position the toes are rotated out. When the bottoms of the feet and the lower legs are in an almost vertical position they kick back with force. When the feet are being flexed they push the water back.

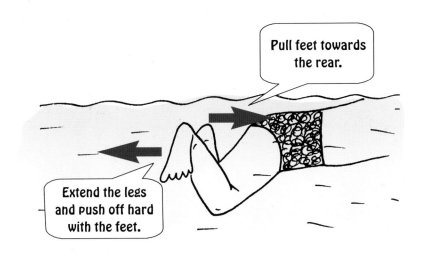

The elbows point forward.

The arms

The arms move out, then down and back. Before the upper arms reach shoulder level the hands and underarms are brought to the inside, while the elbows point forward. The hands nearly touch under the chin. Then the arms are quickly extended and the shoulders move forward along with the arms.

Breathing

Quick deep breaths are taken as the hands and underarms are brought to the inside. Only the head is lifted slightly. During the arm extension the face is on the water and the breath is released evenly through the nose and mouth.

Lift your head and inhale quickly and deeply.

Put your face on the water and exhale slowly and evenly through your mouth and nose.

You can review **the entire movement** on the following pages.

The sequence of movement for the breaststroke

Push off from the wall with your feet and glide, while exhaling through the mouth and nose. The hands are rotated out to *catch the water*.

Now bend the arms slightly and move them to the outside. The head slowly comes back up.

Forcefully pull your arms down and back until they are at shoulder level and the elbows point forward.

Now quickly bring your arms close to your body, while you bend your knees and pull your heels into your rear. The hands are under the chin. The head comes out of the water for breathing. Inhale deeply through the mouth.

Rotate your feet out and pull your toes in toward your knees. The knees are approximately hip-width apart, the feet a little farther. The head slowly moves back down. The face goes in the water to exhale.

Push off hard with your feet. At the same time extend your arms and push your shoulders forward. Legs, feet, arms and hands are extended while you glide. Exhale forcefully through the mouth and nose.

What you really have to pay attention to when you do the breaststroke

In the breaststroke the head is a little higher than the rear. You sit in the water like a flying boat. The shoulders are straight and not moving up or down. Your arm- and leg movements are steady and even. Don't forget to breathe!

The kick

- Pull both heels to your rear at the same time.
- The feet are rotated so the toes point to the outside.
- Push off hard with your feet.

The arm pull

Don't pull your arms too far back; only to just under your shoulders. Then quickly pull your arms in toward your body. Your palms are flat as you extend your arms.

Keep your fingers closed so your hand can act as a shovel and push the water out of the way.

Tips

The following are some important tips you can get from your swimming instructor, your mom, your dad, your grandmother, or someone else.

- [ ] Shoulders are horizontal! The body is straight, the hips steady!
- [ ] The rear stays under water!
- [ ] Look straight ahead, eyes above the surface of the water!
- [ ] Move both legs evenly!
- [ ] Pull your heels to your rear at the same time, don't jerk!
- [ ] Don't pull your knees under your stomach!
- [ ] Toes to the outside and to the knees!
- [ ] The lower legs kick back fast and hard!
- [ ] Push off the water with the bottoms of your feet!
- [ ] Extend your legs all the way!
- [ ] Move your legs in a semi circle!
- [ ] Bend the arms as you pull them through!
- [ ] Don't let your elbows go past your shoulders!
- [ ] Palms are open, fingers together! Knees together!
- [ ] Pull your hands sideways, back and down!
- [ ] No stopping when your arms are under your body!
- [ ] Extend the arms all the way, moving the shoulders forward with the arms!
- [ ] Inhale deeply when your arms come together under your body!
- [ ] Exhale completely into the water while you extend the arms!
- [ ] Do the kick as you extend the arms!
- [ ] Pull the legs in during the final part of the arm pull!

With a pencil check those tips which are particularly important to you. Once a tip isn't needed any more because you are doing it correctly, you can erase that check mark.

Anyone who wants to help you with your swimming needs to watch you carefully and notice if you make mistakes. Don't get upset, but appreciate the advice. It is meant to help you, not hurt you!

Carefully look at these drawings. What are these children doing wrong? We drew circles around the areas where you will find the mistakes.

1

2

3

4

5

6

7

8

How to practice

Did you look at the drawings of the sequence of movement in your swimming book? Your swimming instructor or your parents can also show you the movements. Now you will need to practice lots and lots so you can get really good.

First try practicing with your arms and legs separately. It will be less confusing like that. Once you have mastered that try doing them together.

Land exercises

Do the arm and leg movements very slowly while standing up, sitting down on the edge of the pool, or lying down on a bench. Pay attention to the proper hand and foot positions. Careful, don't fall off!

You can also do these exercises at home.

Water exercises

This is how you can practice the leg movements in the water:
- Hold on to the edge of the pool or the ladder.
- Hold on to a kick board, barbells, or a water noodle.
- Push off the edge of the pool with your feet and assume the glide position. Your arms are extended in front or held against your body.

Don't forget to breathe evenly during all these exercises, or you'll get winded very quickly.

This is how you can practice the arm movements:

- With your feet hold on to the dividing rope or the ladder rungs.
- Ask someone to hold you in the water.
- Hold a kick board between your legs.
- Push off hard with your feet and try to do the arm movements while you glide.

This is how you can practice the arm and leg movements at the same time:

- Wear a flotation device around your waist. Gradually remove sections from the swimming belt or release some of the air from an inflatable device. Soon you will be able to swim without a flotation aid.
- Push off hard from the edge of the pool. Try to complete as many strokes as you can while you glide.
- Stay calm and don't move hastily.

The dive

To do the breaststroke you can start by standing in the water or holding on to the edge of the pool, and then just go.

But when speed is important the swimmers do a starting dive.

92

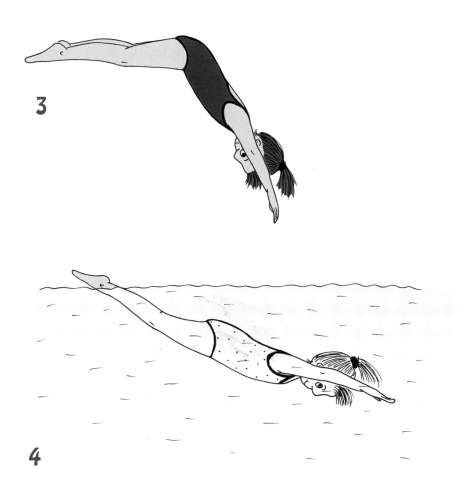

3

4

One version of the starting dive is shown here. Before you dive make sure the water is deep enough.

•••••••••••••••••••••• 10 The Backstroke

Maybe you have learned the breaststroke by now. Most children choose the backstroke as their secondary stroke.

But choosing the backstroke as your primary stroke also has its advantages. You already mastered the interplay of arms and legs by walking and learning to crawl as a baby. Besides, breathing is easier because your face isn't in the water.

Again without a hitch, it's true,
the flying boat position works for you!

Just like the breaststroke swimmer the backstroke swimmer lies in the water at a slight angle.

How to do the backstroke – the technique

The backstroke has an alternating stroke. Both arms and legs are moved alternately. The body lies in the water at an angle like a flying boat. The rear is lower than the shoulders. The eyes are focused on the feet.

The legs

The legs alternate while moving continuously up and down. The powerful kick starts at the hip and moves to the thigh. The legs stay relaxed. The toes are rotated in slightly as the leg comes up, but they stay straight as the leg goes down. The knees should not break the water surface.

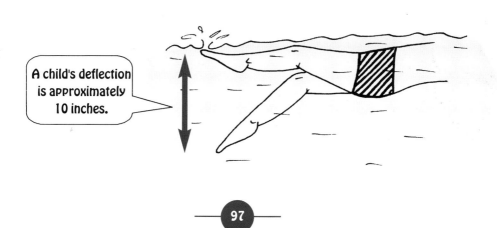

A child's deflection is approximately 10 inches.

The arms

The arms alternate while moving continuously next to the body. The arm is extended and enters the water close to the head. As soon as the arm enters the water and feels the resistance of the water the elbow is bent at a nearly right angle, and then extends again as it approaches the thigh. The flat palm pushes against the water. Once the arm leaves the water at the thigh and circles backwards above the water, it is again extended but relaxed.

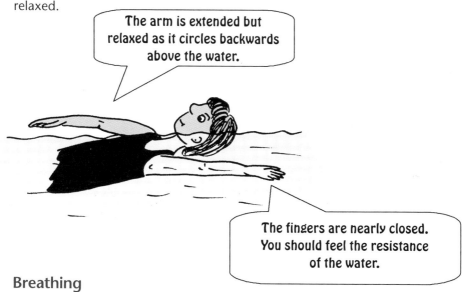

Breathing

Since the face is always above water breathing is possible anytime. A breathing rhythm has to be practiced so regular breathing isn't forgotten. Choose a moment for inhaling and one for exhaling.

For example: Inhale while the right arm rotates, and exhale while the left arm rotates.

You can review the **entire movement** on the following pages.

The sequence of movement for the backstroke

The left hand, led by the pinkie, enters the water first. The arm must immediately catch the water.

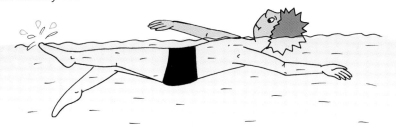

As you push the left arm down to the side the right arm leaves the water.

Bend the elbow and push off hard against the water. The hand leads the movement.

Quickly move your hand to the thigh.

The left arm leaves the water when it reaches the thigh.

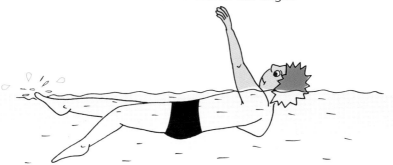

Now extend your arm, but keep it relaxed as you circle it nearly straight back above the water.

The legs move continuously. You will kick your legs six times during one complete arm movement.

What you really have to pay attention to when you do the backstroke

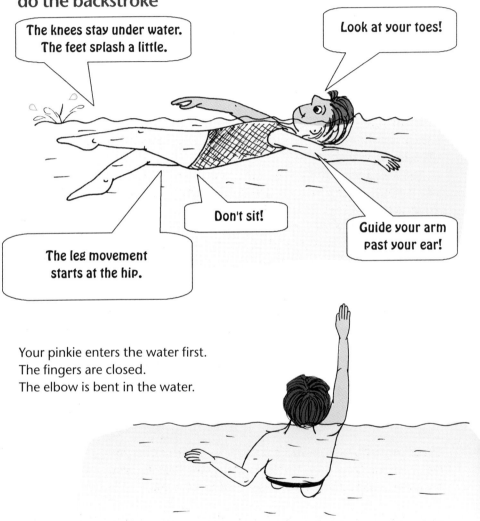

The knees stay under water. The feet splash a little.

Look at your toes!

Don't sit!

The leg movement starts at the hip.

Guide your arm past your ear!

Your pinkie enters the water first.
The fingers are closed.
The elbow is bent in the water.

Due to the arm movement the body rolls slightly side to side. Be careful not to roll too much.

Here are a few important tips you can get from your swimming instructor, your mom, your dad, your grandmother, or someone else.

- ☐ Don't sit! Keep your rear to the water surface.
- ☐ Shoulders up!
- ☐ Don't rock!
- ☐ Don't turn side to side!
- ☐ Keep your body straight!
- ☐ Look at your toes!
- ☐ Keep your head still and relaxed, and don't turn it to the side!
- ☐ Thighs move with the legs!
- ☐ Keep your knees under water and don't bend them too much!
- ☐ Keep your ankles relaxed and your toes long, and don't "bicycle"!
- ☐ Toes are turned in on the up-kick!
- ☐ Toes break the water surface, making waves!
- ☐ Leg movement is well-rounded, not tremulous!
- ☐ Continuous arm movement!
- ☐ Alternating arm pull!
- ☐ Powerful arm pull, moving the pinkie past the thigh!
- ☐ Emphasis on the final push-off without pulling too deep!
- ☐ Feel the water's resistance, don't spread your fingers, and don't cant your hands!
- ☐ Arms are extended and the upper arm passes close to the ear!
- ☐ Breathe regularly!
- ☐ Determine on which arm pull to breathe!
- ☐ Exhale strongly and completely!

Check those tips which are particularly important to you with a pencil. Once a tip isn't needed anymore because you are doing it correctly, you can erase that check mark.

Anyone who wants to support you with your swimming needs to watch you carefully and notice when you make mistakes. Don't get upset, but appreciate the advice. It is meant to help you, not hurt you!

Can you see what these children are doing wrong with the backstroke? We drew circles around the areas where you will find the mistakes.

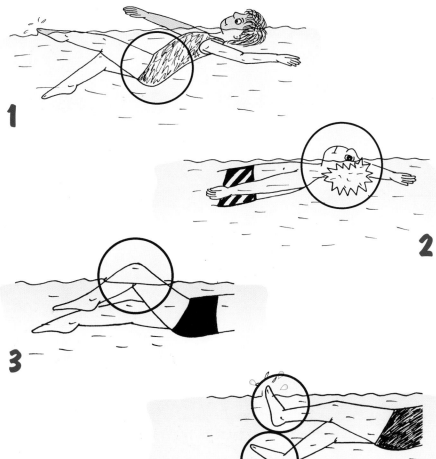

1

2

3

4

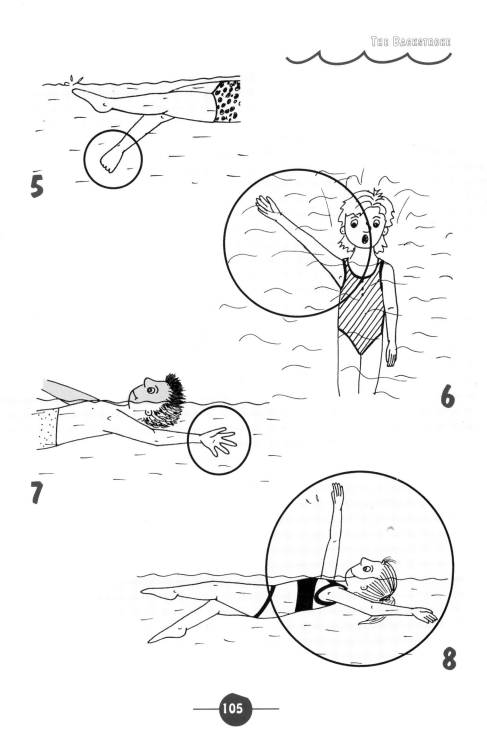

Dolly and Speedster practice the backstroke ...!

How to practice

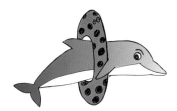

After someone has explained the backstroke movements to you, you will need to practice them over and over again. But to keep your arms and legs from flailing wildly you will need the proper rhythm. That's not easy!

At first practice only with your legs, and after that only with your arms. This will be less confusing. Once you are doing both well you can try doing them at the same time.

Land exercises

Do the arm and leg movements very slowly while standing up, sitting on the edge of the pool, or lying down on a bench. Pay attention to the proper hand and foot positions.

You can also do these exercises at home.

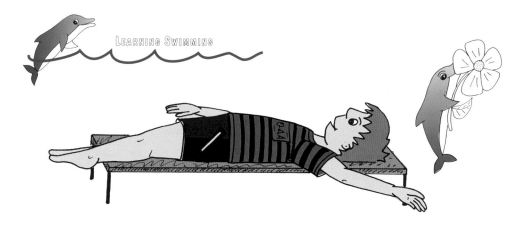

Water exercises

This is how you can practice the kick in the water:
- Sit down on the pool steps in the water.
- With your hands hold on to the edge of the pool, the spillway, or the ladder.
- Place a kickboard under your head and hold on to the barbells.
- Push off from the edge of the pool and get into the glide position. The arms are back, or against your body.

Don't forget to breathe evenly during all these exercises, or you'll get winded very quickly.

This is how you can practice the arm pull in the water:

- With your feet hold on to the spillway or the ladder.
- Ask someone to hold you in the water.
- Push off hard with your feet and try doing the arm movements as you glide.

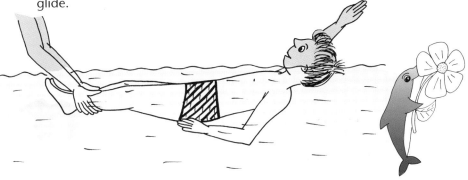

This is how you can practice the arm pull and kick at the same time:

- Put a swimming belt or some other floatation device around your waist and do a few of the arm and leg movements.
- Place a kickboard under your head and hold on to it with just one hand. The other arm practices together with the legs. Then switch arms.
- Push off hard, glide, and do as many arm and leg movements as you can.

The backstroke take-off

In swimming the command "Start" or a whistle blow signals the start of a race. But how do you get the fastest start? There is a special way to start the backstroke.

1

With your hands hold on to the edge of the pool, the spillway, or the ladder, and set your feet against the wall. Your chin rests on your chest.

2

As soon as the command to start is given push off hard and extend your legs. The arms move back.

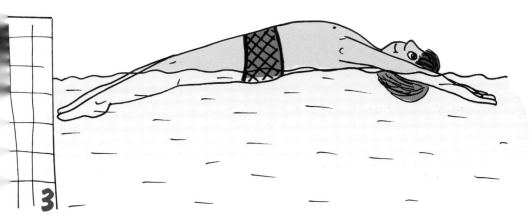

3

The momentum and your extended body let you glide through the water for a while. Start with the kick and then add the arms.

...........11 KEEPING THINGS STRAIGHT

Playing in the water and swimming are fun. You can have lots of fun at an indoor pool, and when the sun is warm you can go to an outdoor pool or to the beach. But to make sure the day is a happy one, children and adults alike must act appropriately and be considerate.

Maybe you have heard about how someone might get hurt in the water, or even drown. On the next few pages we have written down some important things to help you stay safe in the water.

Rules – at the pool

Every pool is required to post a sign stating the pool rules. Look for that sign at your pool and read those rules. Ask someone to explain anything you don't understand.

As a pool guest you have to behave as a guest.

Use the facilities and equipment carefully. Try not to damage or soil anything. That will make the pool a better place for everyone.

Don't wear your street shoes on the pool deck to keep it clean.

Go to the locker room and shower thoroughly before you get in the pool. And remember to use the restroom. You wouldn't want to swim in dirty water either.

Don't bring food or beverages to the pool deck. Crumbs will dirty the water. Never bring glass bottles as they can break and cause injury.

Speedster, come get in the shower!

I'm getting in the pool in a second. I'll get clean there.

What do you think about Speedster? Is he right?

Be considerate of the other pool guests. Don't do anything that might disturb, anger, or even hurt someone.

- Only jump in where it is allowed. Be careful not to jump on top of someone.

- Make sure you don't bump into other people while you are swimming.

- Don't push another pool guest into the water or hold someone under water. That person might get frightened or swallow water.

Don't do anything that might cause you harm.

Never get in the pool alone if you don't know how to swim.

If you are a beginning swimmer, only get in deep water with an adult. If you become unsure or tired you have immediate help.

Walk and don't run along the edge of the pool. You might slip and fall down.

Pool guests who don't adhere to the rules may be asked to leave. If they behaved inconsiderately they may not be allowed to come back.

The lifeguard

Have you ever noticed the lifeguards at the pool? They watch everyone in the pool and make sure that guests follow the pool rules. Everyone must listen to the lifeguards or other pool staff!

The lifeguards make sure that nothing happens to any of the pool guests. They sit at the edge of the pool or walk around, and keep an eye on all the swimmers. Lifeguards are good and fast swimmers and know the life saving techniques. If a child or an adult call out for help or someone is in danger the lifeguard springs into action.

Never call for help as a joke. The lifeguard would rush to your side and might not see someone else who really is in danger.

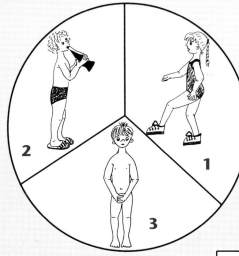

These children are at the pool. Look at the pictures. What are they doing wrong?

Which of these things don't belong at the pool? Cross out the items you should leave at home.

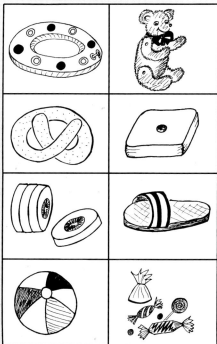

Let's go to the lake or the ocean

Julie has passed her first swimming test. "Finally", she thinks, "I can swim anywhere I like!"

The following Saturday is a warm and sunny day and the family decides to go to the lake. Julie puts on her swimming suit and immediately jumps into the deep water. But what's this? The cold water shocks her and she can barely move her arms and legs. And then a wave hits her right in her face. Fortunately Daddy is there and holds on to her. "Well, you master-swimmer," he says. "It's not quite as easy as you thought!"

 *Once you have passed your swimming test you may get in the deep water. But that doesn't mean that there is no danger. You will need to practice swimming in cold or moving water. Always be careful in unfamiliar waters.*

Some important rules for swimming

If you are fit and healthy
there is no reason not to get in the water.

•

Check the water temperature before you get in
or you might be in for a shock.

•

Swimming on a really full stomach
might not feel very good.

•

If you are really hot from playing in the sun
don't jump directly into cold water.

•

Always pay attention to buoys, barriers, and weather markers.
They are there to keep you out of danger.

•

Even if your friends are having fun on a blow-up raft,
you could easily slide off and drown
if you don't know how to swim.

•

Always tell someone when you are getting in the water.
If something should happen help won't be far away.

•

Beginning swimmers should not play
where older children jump and dive.

•

If you get cold in the water you'll tire quickly.
Get out of the water and dry off.

First aid

Of course we want you to have a happy and carefree swimming experience. Adhering to the rules will help you stay safe, but if something ever does happen it's good to be prepared.

Emergency rescue

If you see a swimmer in trouble you have to help

- Throw something in the water he or she can hold on to (life saver, kickboard, water noodle, or something similar).
- Get help! Tell the lifeguard or another adult.
- If you are safely on land you can hold a rope or a stick out to the swimmer.
- If you are a beginning swimmer don't try to swim to the victim. You are not yet strong and steady enough. You could easily drown while trying to safe someone else.

If you are the one in trouble

- Stay calm! You'll lose too much strength by flailing around. Try to hold on to something.
- Try to get the attention of other swimmers by shouting or waving your arms.

If you get a cramp

If your fingers, feet, or legs get really stiff you probably have a cramp. That can happen if you have been really exerting yourself, or the water is too cold. A cramp can be dangerous because you are not able to move properly. But you can help yourself.

When you get a **finger cramp** your fingers suddenly get really stiff and hurt.

Alternate between: opening your hand wide and making a fist.

If your **toes** are spread and stiff that's where the cramp is.

Alternate between: pushing your toes down and relaxing them.

When your thigh gets really hard and hurts you have a thigh cramp.

Alternate between: bringing your heel to your rear and straightening the leg.

If you get a **calf cramp:**

pull hard on your big toe.

Now you can do some exercises at home.

Speedster loves to gently rock on the waves on a blow-up raft. Sometimes the waves get so big that he falls off. But that's ok because Speedster is an awesome swimmer. He has been practicing for a long time.

It is particularly important for beginning swimmers not to get themselves needlessly into dangerous situations. Blow-up rafts, blow-up boats, or surf-boards can be very dangerous. They can easily turn over and fall on top of the swimmer.

Dolly and Speedster are having a race. Which one swims to the ball and which one to the duck?

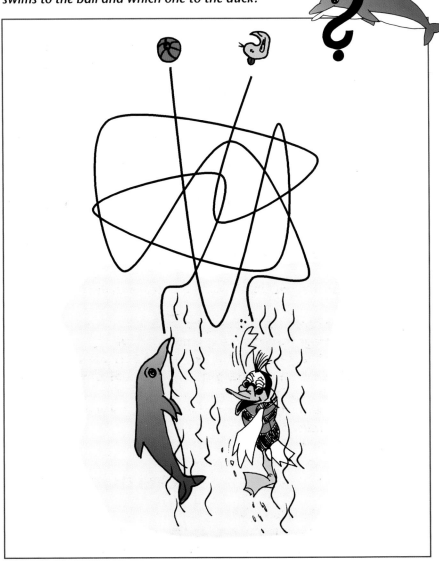

............12 SOLUTIONS AND ANSWERS

P. 31   The word water makes us think of: wet, warm, cold, wavy, ship, ocean, swimming, washing, shower, pool, swimming suit, rubber ducky, fishing, diving, dangerous, fun, vacation, rain, rubber boots, drinking …

P. 32   Water ball, water faucet, water snake, water drop, water slide.

P. 34   You will see a whirlpool and the ball is swirling in the vortex.

P. 44   Frog, large fish, small fish, three tadpoles, turtle, large duck, duckling.

P. 44   Dolly is behind the cattails.

P. 51   You should not take the stuffed toy cat into the water.

P. 86/87   1 The body lies too low in the water.
           2 The legs are not moving simultaneously.
           3 The knees are pulled in too close to the stomach.
           4 The feet are not extended. The face needs to be in the water while exhaling.
           5 The foot breaks the water surface and the foot is slapping the water surface.
           6 The arms are too low and too far back.
           7 The fingers are not closed.
           8 The elbows are too high. They break the water surface.

P. 104/105 1 The rear is too low.
           2 The head is too far back and the eyes are not on the feet.
           3 The knees are too high. They break the water surface.

4 The feet are not extended.

5 One foot is turned in. This is called scissor kick.

6 The arm is too far to the outside and not close to the body.

7 The fingers are not closed.

8 The arm movement is not uniform.

P. 114   All pool guests must shower thoroughly before getting in the pool. If everyone was like Speedster the pool would be full of dirty water. Would you want to swim in that?

P. 116   **1** Bringing glass bottles to the pool is not allowed. People could get badly cut if a bottle broke. Besides, you should eat and drink after you are done swimming.

2 Street shoes are not allowed on the pool deck.

3 This child must have forgotten to bring a swimming suit. Proper swimming attire is mandatory at all pools.

P. 116

P. 122   Dolly swims to the ball and Speedster swims to the duck.

....................................13 Let's talk

Dear Parents, Dear Grandparents, Dear Siblings, Dear Friends ...!

Learning to swim is an important developmental step in the lives of our little ones. The long caption suggests just how many people want to help our children learn to swim. In the book we sometimes refer only to the big people.

It is important that we recognize that swimming is initially not just a recreational activity or one of many sports, but that everyone must be able to swim. Aside from the many health-related aspects swimming has lifesaving relevance. If our children can swim and move around in the water safely we don't have to fear for their lives. It makes our time spent on, in, and near the water much more pleasurable.

What's the right way?

Literally jumping right into the cold water may not be the most suitable approach for taking away our children's timidity of water, or to foster joy in swimming or maybe eventually swimming as a sport. We try to gradually get our children used to the wet environment. Usually it begins with playing in the bath tub, later in a baby pool or in swimming lessons. We have listed some options for this in Chapter 7.

As we have outlined in Chapter 8 "The basic Skills", learning water safety and floating skills

are pre-conditions to learning to swim. Surely you will find many exercises and other possibilities for your children. It really does not matter whether you start with the breaststroke or the backstroke. Swimming instructors may have preferences since both strokes offer different advantages.

Over time, various swimming techniques and learning methods have been developed. We have listed those techniques which we consider to be the best and most suitable. Of course there are different opinions on this, just like there are on any topic. If your opinions or the opinions of your swimming instructor are different from those favored in this book, then that is perfectly alright.

Are those dear relatives really good instructors?

Anyone who has the desire, the time, and the opportunity to teach his or her child to swim will have lots of fun doing so. It is an opportunity for bonding and an ego booster. But it is also possible that the closeness and affectionate interaction can be an impediment at swimming lessons. Would you be able to be firm and consistent when things aren't going so well? In a group setting with a teacher, a child would be less likely to say "I don't want to do this anymore!", or "I won't do that!"

Swimming lessons are done in group settings, or as private or semi-private lessons. With an experienced swimming instructor and a group lesson, you will see your children make quick progress.

No pain, no gain and no success without a goal

Do you remember your little one taking its first steps? They were so wobbly and clumsy. There was much pride and progress but there were also set-backs resulting in tears and in dirty and bruised knees. Today you can hardly remember all that practicing when you look at your little speed-demon.

It's much like learning to swim. No one is a perfect swimmer at birth, but rather requires much practice and diligence. Of course it's not always fun right away. You swallow lots of water, your eyes burn, and sometimes your arms and legs ache. While practicing it often happens that the initial delight and enthusiasm give way to tears, dejection, and defiance.

The child needs to know: What's it all about? Why am I working so hard? Talk to your child about the main objective, which is learning to swim. Ask him or her about the benefits of being able to swim, and together try to set *goals*.

Why do you want to learn to swim?

- *I want to be able to play at the pool with my friends.*
- *My friends all know how to swim.*
- *I don't want to be afraid of the deep water anymore.*
- *I don't want to drown.*
- *I want to be a really fast swimmer and become a World Champion.*
- *Moving in the water is fun and healthy.*
- *Everyone needs to know how to swim.*

If you practice with your child you can set *small or partial goals* for each lesson along with the *main goal*. Together with your child plan exercises that should be accomplished. You will find examples in Chapter 8 "The basic Skills". Once the exercise has been accomplished your child may

color the flower. Partial goals can also be set for learning the breaststroke and the backstroke. You probably have some good ideas of your own for child-appropriate rewards.

If a child knows why it is working on something he or she will be more likely to persevere. It's alright if occasionally something doesn't go as well as expected. Just get up and try again! Regresses during the learning process are totally normal and should not be discouraging.

Don't expect more of your child than he or she is capable of at the moment. Comparing your child with other children in his or her age group is also not advisable. Children at that age vary greatly in their level of maturity. Rather focus on your own child and praise his or her advances.

How to use this little book

This book is intended as a kind of reference book, diary, and workbook for the child itself. It offers valuable information about everything to do with swimming. It is intended to help your child learn to swim and a little beyond.

In their personal copy of the swimming book the children will be able to color pictures, solve puzzles, paste photos, and record their advances. Since most beginning swimmers are pre-school children they will need your help with the text. Look at the pictures and exercise examples with your child. You know your child and how to best work with him or her.

Let us provide the necessary ideas. Choose those exercises from the book that are feasible and suitable for your conditions. There are many sensible exercises for getting used to the water, water safety, and water familiarity. By gently introducing your child to the water you can take away his or her timidity. Soon scaredy-cats will turn into little water rats.

The family members' role during swimming lessons

If you have opted for swimming lessons you should leave the work in the pool to the swimming instructor. Parents shouting or gesticulating wildly are disruptive and distract the children. The children's escorts should only participate if the instructor asks them to do so. However, it is important that children are accompanied, particularly pre-school age children.

Mom, I'm ready!

They still require help with changing and showering, and praise, comfort, and encouragement from Mom, Dad, Grand-mom, or other loved ones is very important. Share the joy over learning achievements and dispel any doubts about a success-ful completion.

Everyone will make it!

129

What a children's swimming instructor must have

Incentive, praise, comfort, and encouragement for everyone.

Technical knowledge and organizational skills.

Solutions to their problems.

A soft spot for children.

The ability to convey the fun and joy in the sport.

Skill in dealing with children.

Be knowledgeable about children's physical characteristics and developmental phases.

Good communication with parents.

Dear Swimming Instructor!

Surely you'll agree with us that it is a great feeling to see these little guys standing before you, their faces full of curiosity and their eyes wide with anticipation. They all want to learn how to swim and that responsibility now lies with you.

But each of these children is different from the other. There are the anxious ones and the brave ones, the talented ones and the less talented ones, the precocious ones and the late bloomers. Each child is a little individual with his or her individual background and developmental history, with hopes and desires, and existential orientation and needs. All of them are worthy of our attention, our care, and our love.

The more a swimming instructor is able to relate to his or her beginning swimmers, empathizes with them, is accessible to them, and inspires them, the more effective he or she will be. The instructor must encourage them and listen to them, understand them, praise and comfort them – in short, he or she must have a soft spot for children. Sometimes the instructor needs to put the brakes on a hot head or issue a reprimand. But he or she always does so with respect for the little individual.

The value of this little book

Books are no substitute for many years of poolside experience with beginning swimmers. No drawing or photo can measure up to an instructor's demonstration. This book can not take the place of the swimming instructor, but it can accompany the children as they learn to swim, and provide some assistance to the instructor.

With parents doing lots of preliminary exercises in the bathtub and at the pool the fear of water can be taken away. Children will become more comfortable in the water and more safety-conscious, which helps them get off to an easier start at swimming lessons and makes the swimming instructor's job a little easier.

This book is meant to inspire parents, grandparents, and siblings to get involved because without their help swimming lessons, particularly at the pre-school age, are unrealizable. They get a chance to support their little ones in the learning process.

This book offers children opportunities for being involved with swimming away from the pool. They can look up things they just learned and get suggestions for exercises at home.

This book is meant to be a personal companion to children learning to swim. Let them make entries, give them small tasks to do at home, and take a group photo to paste in the book. An active involvement with swimming promotes enjoyment and interest in the sport. And soon you may see your little beginning swimmers on a swim team.

Technique, methodology, time flow, as well as exercise progression are of course the swimming instructor's responsibility. We welcome any critical commentaries or suggestions.

We wish you lots of fun and enjoyment with your little charges!

PHOTO AND ILLUSTRATION CREDITS

Cover design: Jens Vogelsang
Illustrations: Katrin Barth
Cover photo: Regina Weitz
Photos (interior): Katrin Barth, Birgit Küspert, Manfred Sendelbeck,
                    Regina Weitz

Barth/Dietze
Training ... Swimming

If you have learned to swim and you want to do more, it's time to start swim training. This book will help you with that. It describes the techniques involved in the different strokes from start, to turn, to finish, and tells you how to correct mistakes to become an accomplished swimmer. As in the previous book "Learning Swimming", the dolphin girl "Dolly" will be at your side, offering support and advice.

You will find out how to improve your fitness level specifically for swimming, how training on land can be helpful, and how to prepare for a swim meet. In addition to all of the swimming information you will also find useful tips on nutrition, equipment, and life saving in the water.

The easy to read text and descriptive illustrations, as well as the many opportunities to make personal entries, make this book an important training companion.

About 152 pages, full-color print
15 photos, numerous illustrations
Paperback, 5^3/4" x 8^1/4"
ISBN 1-84126-145-9
c. £ 9.95 UK / $ 14.95 US
$ 20.95 CDN / € 14.90

MEYER & MEYER Sport | sales@m-m-sports.com | www.m-m-sports.com

MEYER
& MEYER
SPORT